HOW
ON
EARTH
DO
WE
RECYCLE
GLASS?

German
glassmaking,
about 1300.

HOW ON EARTH DO WE RECYCLE

GLASS?

JOANNA RANDOLPH ROTT
and
SELI GROVES

Illustrations by

ART SEIDEN

THE MILLBROOK PRESS
Brookfield, Connecticut

The prints and photos included are courtesy of
State of California, Dept. of Conservation: pp. 6, 19, 21;
The Corning Museum of Glass: pp. 10, 11;
Anchor Hocking: p. 13;
New Jersey Glass Recycling Association: p. 15;
Waste Management, Inc.: p. 17;
Carolinas Glass Recycling Program: pp. 18, 25.

Typography and electronic composition by Essentially Visual.

Produced in association with **STEARN/KNUDSEN & CO.**

Printed in the United States of America
5 4 3 2 1
Library of Congress Cataloging-in-Publication Data
Rott, Joanna Randolph, 1934-
How on earth do we recycle glass? / by Joanna Randolph Rott & Seli Groves;
illustrated by Art Seiden.
p.   cm.
Includes index.
Summary: Describes the making of glass and the problems caused by
glass waste. Also gives suggestions for ways of using discarded glass.
ISBN 1-56294-141-0
1. Glass waste—Recycling—Juvenile literature. [1. Glass waste—Recycling.] I.
Groves, Seli. II. Seiden, Art, ill. III. Title.
TP859.7.R68 1992
363.72'82—dc20
91-24241 CIP AC

This book is printed on recycled paper.

CONTENTS

Join a recycling team
for fun and profit
and help
clean up the
community, too.

1 HOW ON EARTH DO WE RECYCLE GLASS?

Reflections on Glass

Think about it—without glass, we might never have gone into space or found the cures for many diseases or developed light bulbs that turn darkness into light. We could never see exactly what we look like, so no artist could paint a self-portrait. We'd have no windshields or window panes. And we would still be waiting for someone to invent spyglasses and eyeglasses, not to mention the barometer and the thermometer and, of course, the telescope and the microscope.

Glass is one of our most important products and, fortunately, one of the most gentle to our environment. Unlike most plastics, it won't linger in a garbage dump beyond the point at which even the cockroach (which is supposed to outlast us all) becomes extinct. That's because plastics are made of petroleum and other materials that resist nature's normal degrading process, while glass is degradable. This means that it will break down into its natural elements. Another advantage of glass is that it can be continually reused and recycled.

The more we learn about glass and how vital it is to our lives and to our economy and ecology, the more we appreciate this remarkable and very old substance and the part it has played throughout the history of civilization.

From Fiery Volcanoes to Fiber Optics

Millions of years before people started making glass, nature was creating it within her own fiery furnaces—volcanoes. The heat that escapes from an erupting volcano is hot enough to melt everything it covers, including silicates, the substances from which glass is made.

Silicates make up most of the earth's outer surface. They are formed from various types of rocks and minerals such as quartz, calcium, magnesium, talc, asbestos, and so on. Some silicates contain the skeletons or shells of creatures that lived millions of years ago. Some were once whole mountains that the wind and water eroded into fine grains over millions of years. Others are the dust of ancient seas, dried up remnants of their underwater hills and valleys.

Silicates make up most of the earth's outer crust.

Since silicates are the most plentiful of all naturally occurring substances on this planet, you may wonder if you've ever seen them. The answer is definitely YES; silicates are all around you. You probably played in boxes filled with them when you were a toddler. You may have built castles by the sea made of silicates. You may even have set miniature cactus plants in pots filled with silicates on your windowsill, and no doubt you've seen films of camels with their big, splayed feet plodding over large expanses of shifting silicates. If you suspect we're talking about something as common as sand, you're absolutely right.

The way nature makes glass from sand, or silicates, is really quite simple. The volcanic heat fuses, or melts, the silicates. As they cool, they harden into glass. The most common type of naturally formed glass is called obsidian. Long before people started making glass, they were shaping obsidian formations into jewelry.

Nature also produces glass from a type of quartz called rock crystal. Very fine, very clear manufactured glass is called rock crystal because it resembles the clear, transparent beauty of the natural material.

The First Glassmakers. No one knows exactly when people started making glass. It is likely that the process was discovered by chance in Egypt, about 4,000 years ago. According to one story, it all began in the workshop of an Egyptian metalworker and his son. The man earned his living by heating pieces of metal so that he could bend and reshape them into other objects. He needed a very hot fire to do this. It was his son's job to feed the fire with reeds and cow manure (wood was in short supply) and to fan it with large palm fronds, the ancient Egyptian equivalent of a bellows.

The father had to leave for a while. It was a very warm day and, with all the fanning and fueling, the boy soon fell asleep. When the father returned, he woke his son with an angry shake and pointed to the firepit. The fire had gone out and would have to be started over again. It would take hours for it to become hot enough to bend metal. As the two cleaned the ashes out of the firepit, they picked up several hard, shining objects from the bottom. They were dazzled and delighted to see them sparkle in the sunlight. These glass pieces were formed when the hot fire fused the sand in the firepit. When the fire went out, the melted sand cooled, hardening into bits of gleaming glass.

In any case, by 1500 B.C., 500 years after they discovered glass-making, the Egyptians were shaping molten glass into vases, cups, jewelry, and art works, and selling them all over the known world.

Innovations in Glass. Artisans in ancient Rome made windowpanes, mirrors, prisms, and magnifying glass. They also developed methods of producing colored glass, which they shaped and carved into jewelry. Craftsmen fused and molded long, thin rods into colorful, decorative glassware.

Glassmaking became such an important part of the economy of Venice in the 14th century that Venetian glassmakers were forbidden to tell anyone the secrets of their craft.

In the 1500s, the Dutch perfected ways to shape thick chunks of glass so that when you looked through them, everything appeared to be much bigger. The Netherlands became the center of the optical glass industry. The Dutch produced eyeglasses that were carefully ground to fit the wearer's need. This led the Dutch to pioneer the development of both the telescope and the microscope. The telescope started us on our journey into outer space. The microscope opened up an inner world filled with all sorts of invisible creatures, including bacteria. This soon led to the discovery of the first known causes, and subsequent cures, of many diseases.

Dutch settlers built the first glassmaking factory in America in 1608, and by the 1750s, glassmaking had become one of America's most important industries. The United States continues to be a major producer of new forms and uses for this wonderful material. Among these products are things we recognize at first glance, such as windows, eyeglasses, and light bulbs, and others, less obvious, which originate from glass. For example, fiberglass is actually strands of fine glass that can be turned into anything from fabrics and roofing materials to automobile bodies and boat hulls.

Another advance in the use of glass is in fiber optics technology, where pulses of light transmit thousands of messages through bundles of fine glass filaments, each as thin as a hair. Light and glass carry communications around the world and into space, or even around the corner when you telephone your best friend.

The Glassmaking Process

The process for making glass today is much the same as it was when the Egyptians started glassmaking. It always begins with silicates and high heat. In the past, however, glassmakers set up their facilities near sandpits or other silicate deposits. Today, it is no longer necessary to work near a silicate source since the material can be transported anywhere. Long before recycling waste materials became an ecological necessity, the people who worked in glasshouses (the sites where glass is made) reprocessed their glass all the time. They did this because it is essential to use some waste glass, called cullet, to make good new glass.

A typical glass-blowing factory, Brooklyn, 1877.

Cullet is added and melted together with mixtures of silicates and other substances that give special qualities to different types of glass. Some of these substances are lead, which adds brilliance and weight; barium, which is used for glass optical materials such as eyeglasses and telescopes; and boron, an element that combines with silicates to produce a heat-resistant glass called borosilicate.

A type of borosilicate glass with which many of us are familiar is called Pyrex. Corning Glass came out with Pyrex pots and dishes back in 1915. They can go into a hot oven (some can even be placed directly on a burner) without breaking. These make perfect food containers for the microwave oven. A variation of borosilicate glass is called pyroceramics, which is used in the manufacture of nose cones on space vehicles because of its ability to withstand the extremely high temperatures generated during reentry from space into our atmosphere.

In order to produce any of these glass mixtures, the ingredients are fused together in special containers made to withstand high temperatures. When the mixture has melted, impurities that rise to the surface are skimmed off. After the molten glass has cooled down, it is ladled or poured into molds. It may then be pressed or blown into shape. Then, the newly shaped glass is reheated and cooled down slowly, once again, to relieve any stress caused by excessive handling.

Most hollow objects, such as light bulbs, are blown into shape by glassblowing machines. But skilled glassblowers still blow very fine glassware into goblets, vases, or other decorative objects by hand. The glassblower uses a long metal pipe, one end of which is dipped into the molten glass. The glassblower then blows through the pipe until the molten glass starts to turn into what can best be described as a big bubble. When it reaches a certain form and size, it will be shaped and probably reblown, and then molded.

Finally, the finished glass can be cut, etched, engraved, enameled, or painted, resulting in something beautiful to behold.

The Big Breakthrough in Glass. As most of us know, one of the problems with glass is that if it breaks, it can shatter into sharp, dangerous pieces. For years glassmakers tried to find ways to strengthen their glass, but the shattering problem persisted.

One day in 1903, 12 years before Pyrex was developed, a French scientist named Edouard Benedictus was working in his laboratory in Paris, when he dropped a glass beaker full of liquid celluloid that he had planned to use in an experiment. What he saw on the floor, instead of shards of glass, was a beaker whose broken pieces remained stuck to each other like the pieces of a jigsaw puzzle. This accident led to the invention of shatter-proof glass. In time, this new glass would be used for the windshields of cars, trains, and planes and the windows in skyscrapers; and in glass doors, eyeglasses, and furniture—wherever safety was essential.

From Wonder Product to Waste Problem

There was a time, not so long ago, when people rarely threw out anything made of glass. Jars were used and reused until they finally broke. Empty glass jars became containers for storing foods such as flour and pasta on pantry shelves. They were also used to keep leftovers fresh for a day or so in the icebox (where most people kept their perishable foods back when your grandparents were kids) or for a few days in the refrigerator. Jelly makers even sold their products in glass jars that could serve as drinking glasses after the last bit of jelly had been spooned out.

Glass containers can be both useful and decorative.

Milk and beverage bottles were always returned to the milkman or to the store where they were bought, and the customers would redeem their two-cent deposit. Kids often earned money by taking people's empties back to the store. They were allowed to keep part of the returned deposit for their efforts. Milk and cream were always sold in glass bottles until about the 1950s, when waxed paper cartons were introduced. That pleased many people: paper was lighter to carry and didn't break the way glass did.

Unfortunately, the change was not all for the good. Glass is an easy material to reuse, and because it's mostly silicates, it can also be continually recycled. Paper, however, is limited as a reusable and recyclable resource. Waxed paper cartons, for example, cannot be recycled into new paper products. They wind up either in landfills or incinerators, both of which are expensive and may create environmental problems. As cartons replaced glass bottles, they also increased the demand for paper. This, in turn, widened the threat to our forests because more trees were needed in the papermaking process.

Also, unlike glass, even paper that is recyclable cannot be recycled indefinitely. The fibers weaken each time the paper is put through the process, and finally they can no longer be made into new products. Glass, however, is 100 percent recyclable. This means that one pound of waste glass melted in a glass furnace produces one pound of new glass, and will do so each time it's recycled.

In the 1950s, America—and later much of the rest of the industrialized world—would become known as the throwaway society. Advertisements appearing in newspapers and magazines and on billboards along the highways, as well as radio and television commercials, had one message in common: out with the old and in with the new. People were urged to replace whatever they owned with newer products often described as "improved," "bigger," "better," or all three. Ads made it seem unthinkable to keep the same car for more than a couple of years. Old cars, tires, sinks, stoves, and other discarded objects littered the landscape. While some people were alarmed at the growing trend, many ignored the environmental consequences of their increased consumption. They took pride in acquiring the latest products as soon as they

appeared in the stores. Buying more and more products even seemed to make good economic sense, because it kept businesses booming.

The throw-it-out-and-replace-it syndrome reached into every area of life. Glass bottlers stopped offering deposits for the return of empties. They found it more economical to make new glass from cullet broken during the manufacturing process, because they didn't have to spend money to collect, transport, sort, and wash the returned bottles. As a result, the number of unsightly bottles tossed carelessly along roadways increased. Waste glass became part of the household trash brought to landfills, which were quickly filling up. While manufacturing new glass was, at least temporarily, getting cheaper, disposing of it was becoming more expensive.

Making Mountains Out of Landfills. Early in the 1970s, it suddenly became as clear as glass that we were burying ourselves in overflowing landfills. Solid waste was accumulating faster than we could dispose of it. Although it might take quite a while for the excessive dumping to create "new mountain chains" on the landscape, the fact is that 20 years have passed since we recognized the danger, and still we continue to dump our trash into evergrowing piles all over the country. And we're running out of places to put it all.

Since 1970, Pennsylvania has closed over 975 landfills because they were filled to capacity. The remaining 127 were expected to close some time in 1991. Other states are also rapidly running out of landfill space. The Glass Packaging Institute in Washington, D.C., says that trash disposal costs our country more than four billion dollars a year, and costs are going up all the time as landfills close or reach capacity.

It was also in the 1970s that people became increasingly concerned with other environmental problems. Scientists found that bacteria and chemicals from garbage packed into landfills often leached out of the dumped materials and polluted the underground water supply that many communities depended on. Burning waste materials in incinerators contributed to the worsening quality of the air. Wastes that were dumped into the sea caused ecological disasters. Shellfish beds that had thrived for centuries disappeared. Fishermen complained that they had to go farther out to sea to catch fish that were once more plentiful closer to shore. There was no longer any doubt that we were in trouble. People began to ask, "How did we get into this mess?" The answer was very simple: we had developed wasteful habits, and now we had to break those habits. This meant learning how to live wisely with the environment—not wastefully.

Recycling: A National Concern

We hear a lot about recycling as the solution to waste pollution. Fortunately, glass is one of the best materials to work with in the recycling process. In the following pages you'll see what state and local governments, along with private businesses, are doing about it.

A company called Waste Management in Oak Brook, Illinois, is involved in a project called Recycle America. They provide what are called collection and processing services for recyclable materials. There are 253 Recycle America curbside programs for almost 2 million households around the country. For example, in San Jose, California, 175,000 households take part in the curbside recycling service, and in Seattle, Washington, 52,000 households are enrolled. In the smaller community of Clementon, New Jersey, 1,400 households are participating in a recycling program.

Money received from recyclables at this drop-off center will be contributed to charity.

Although the Environmental Protection Agency (EPA) of the federal government doesn't mandate—or require by law—the recycling of glass, they do provide information on recycling to any state or local governmental agency that requests it. The EPA has also set a national goal of recycling 25 percent of all waste materials by 1992. When this goal is met, we'll have learned a lot more about collecting and processing recyclable materials so that we can set the next goal at a much higher percent.

Some states have laws that do make recycling mandatory for their larger cities or communities. For example, in Pennsylvania, there are curbside recycling programs in 414 communities. Communities with a population of ten thousand or more were the first to be required to recycle. This was followed by mandatory programs in communities from five thousand to ten thousand people. Communities under five thousand are given money by the state to set up their own recycling programs. This money comes from a two dollar fee on every ton of waste that goes to a disposal facility.

Massachusetts, Wisconsin, and Rhode Island are among the states that ban glass and other recyclables from being dumped in disposal facilities. This means that instead of becoming part of a mountain of trash, these materials will be recycled to become new products.

Colorado doesn't have a mandatory glass recycling program. But because there's a major bottling company (Coors) in the state, there's a big market for recycled glass bottles, and numerous drop-offs make the collection easy.

There are several ways to get recyclable materials to recycling centers. One is the popular curbside method. In much the same way that folks wrap their garbage and put it out on the street for the trash collectors, they now sort their recyclables and place special containers, provided by either the municipality or the recycler, at the curb for the recycling company's truck to pick up.

In many communities, people take their waste materials to a drop-off center where glass bottles, as well as plastics and cans, are collected. Usually, no payment is received, but the income from the recycled glass goes to the sponsor of the center, which is often the local government or a charitable organization.

A buy-back center: recycling pays.

Young recyclers collect bottles in a California recreation area.

In other places, people bring bottles straight to a buy-back center for payment. The buy-back centers sort and package the materials and resell them to the manufacturers for reprocessing.

Some communities have installed "igloos" in designated areas. These are not designed to make tourists from the Arctic Circle feel more at home. They are fiberglass domes with round holes at the top in which people can deposit their used glass containers.

One of the most vexing solid-waste problems has been discarded glass that litters streets and roadways. Some states have reintroduced deposits for glass containers. At the time of purchase, people are charged a few cents more per bottle; they then receive a refund when they return the empty container. Deposits have been added to cans and plastic bottles, too.

Tips for Recycling Glass

The Office of Recycling, New Jersey Department of Environmental Protection, offers the following tips:

• Store the glass so it can be separated easily at the time of pickup: Keep clear glass separate from green and amber glass. Be sure the glass is free of contaminants (paper, metal, etc.) that could cause problems in the recycling process.

• Local organizations can sponsor community bottle collection drives. They can establish permanent collection points for used container glass and periodic door-to-door pick-up drives to collect bottles and jars from homes.

• Remember: Recycling centers are interested only in container glass (bottles and jars)—no light bulbs, ceramic glass, crystal or drinking glasses; no glass dishes, windshields, windows, plate glass, heat resistant cookware, or clay pots. It's not that they're fussy about the pattern on your pitchers or the design on your dishes. These products contain ingredients that prohibit production of new, high-quality glass containers.

• What about those broken windows? It can be a problem to have them picked up since recycling centers won't accept this kind of glass. For noncontainer waste glass, a call to your state's Department of Environmental Protection or state glass-recycling association should provide a listing of proper agencies. (See Find Out More, p. 59.)

• Redemption prices—the money paid for recyclable waste glass—varies according to location and according to the color and quality of the glass. Both individuals and government agencies can collect redemption fees.

Recycling Pays

Does it really pay manufacturers to use old glass in making new glass? It certainly does! According to a spokesperson for the New Jersey Glass Recycling Association, if the ingredients for making new glass contain

Recycling and processing bottles stimulate new business.

only 10 percent of cullet, or waste glass, that 10 percent would save only 2.5 percent of the energy needed in production. But, if the batch contains 50 percent cullet, the energy saved would be 12.5 percent. That would save a lot of the fuel oil that otherwise would have been used to generate the electricity that fires the furnaces to white-hot temperatures. Also, because the melting point of the newly mixed glass is reached more quickly with the added cullet, the furnace doesn't go through as much stress and will last much longer.

There have been a few hitches in the increased use of recycled glass. A batch of waste glass that contains contaminants such as wood, loose paper, metal, plastics, and ceramics can foul up the glassmaking process. Before producers began using recycled glass from outside their facilities, contaminants were never a problem. With the increasing use of cullet from other sources, even with the most careful sorting, it's possible that some contaminant will slip through the process.

What to do? Well, smart people would invent smart machines to take care of such problems. And that's what's happening right now. A sensor capable of detecting contaminants is being developed and should be in use in a very short time. Handsorting will still be used in the first step of the separation process. The sensor will be used in the final phase.

Plastics still dominate the container industry. But with more efficient means of producing new glass (thanks to recycling), and with plastic costs rising due to higher prices for petroleum (a key ingredient in plastic), bottlers and food packagers are again finding glass an economical container for their products.

Another major problem faced by food producers has been keeping oxygen out of their containers to prevent food from spoiling. One solution requires multi-layers of plastic in the packaging. For example, most of the plastic drink boxes holding single servings of juice, as well as microwaveable plastic containers, may require as many as six layers of plastic to be effective.

However, researchers at a company called Flex Products have found that if they coat containers with a special glass material, they can use fewer plastic liners. Because the new glass-based linings are so thin, they won't impede the recycling of these products into other items such as food and detergent pouches.

As the environmental movement grows, new techniques and technologies for recycling waste products are being developed to deal with the waste problem. But no matter how innovative an idea might be, the most effective method will always be the determination of people to make their recycling programs work.

Share Your Knowledge

Keep a list of environmental topics that you spot when you read the papers or watch the news, or that you discuss in your classroom. Discuss these topics with your parents and friends.

Your parents could find the information quite helpful in their own efforts to make your community more responsive to recycling. It could help them decide on the projects and programs they should vote for, and also give them topics to discuss at town meetings. You and your parents could write letters about your concerns to the editor of a local newspaper or to ecology editors at radio and television stations.

For example, if you read something about glass being an environmentally effective building material, tell your parents. They may raise this at a meeting when new construction is being considered for the community. Or, if new roads are being built in your area, tell your mom and dad that you learned about glassphalt, which may be more economical to use than asphalt. (Glassphalt is made from petroleum and cullet or waste glass; asphalt uses petroleum and gravel.)

When you go shopping with your parents or friends, look for packaging that is friendly to the environment. Choose glass over plastic whenever possible. Ask your parents to write letters to manufacturers suggesting that they use more glass and less plastic in packaging their products.

Suggest to your parents that they take a canvas bag with them when they shop. This will help cut down on the use of both paper and plastic bags.

Tell your parents about the wonderful gifts they can buy for everyone in the family in thrift shops. There are many lovely things for sale at prices far below what they would cost elsewhere. And everyone benefits: consumers get bargain prices; the charitable organizations that usually run these shops earn needed funds; and an object that might have been thrown into the trash heap gets a new lease on life. And, of course, you, your friends, and your parents should keep in mind that when you have something you no longer can use, don't dump it—donate it to a thrift shop.

Get together with your classmates and make it a classroom project to establish a block-by-block or class-by-class ecology watch. Your classroom can be the headquarters for your activities. You might organize a Deposit Volunteer Group to help senior citizens carry their bottles back to the store. Suggest causes to which consumers might want to contribute their refunded deposit money. For example, buy sports equipment for a school team or treat hospitalized children to a party.

Find out what's new in recycling programs in your area. For information, check the region of the country in which you live and contact the office listed next to it. (See Find Out More, p. 61.) Share what you have learned with your teacher and classmates, or others who are interested in working to protect the environment.

Write to glass manufacturers for information on how they recycle old glass and what products they produce from the reclaimed material. For a list of major glass manufacturers, contact the Glass Packaging Institute. (See Find Out More, p. 60.)

Talk to your teacher about setting up class discussions on reusing materials. You might have a show-and-tell or hold a contest in which your classmates bring in new ideas about how to reuse a glass jar, a bottle, a picture frame, or another familiar object .

Exhibit all the recycled glass objects you and your friends produce from the projects described in the following Craft section. Have it written up in your school paper or even in your local newspaper.

Summing Up:
Learning the New 6 R's

Everyone knows that in school we study the 3 R's: "reading, 'riting, and 'rithmetic." Now there are also the 6 R's, and if we're going to succeed in preserving and protecting our environment, we need to learn these new lessons well. We need to

1. *Rethink* our priorities. That means instead of just thinking about how to handle the growing waste problem, we also need to understand that the best way to deal with waste is to produce less of it.

2. *Reduce* the source of waste by using what we already have; stop accumulating what we don't need. One way to do that is to buy more unpackaged foods. Some stores offer coffee, rice, beans, herbs, nuts, cookies, candies, and even pickles in closed bins and barrels. Customers bring clean glass containers to the store, have the shopkeeper weigh out the purchase, and then put it into the right-sized container. Less packaging, less waste!

3. *Reuse* glass products as often as possible. For example, take a jar and use it to hold a prized marble collection, to store leftovers, to mix up a batch of concentrated juice, or to take

back to the store for refills of certain foods. Turn it upside down to make a great cookie cutter, or use it as a vase to hold flowers.

4. *Repair* broken objects to make them useful again and save them from becoming mounting trash heaps around us.

5. *Redeem* deposit bottles before they break and end up as part of the trash pile. Make sure all empty redeemable bottles and jars in your home are carefully washed and stored. Set aside some time each week to take them back to the store.

HOW GLASS BOTTLES ARE RECYCLED

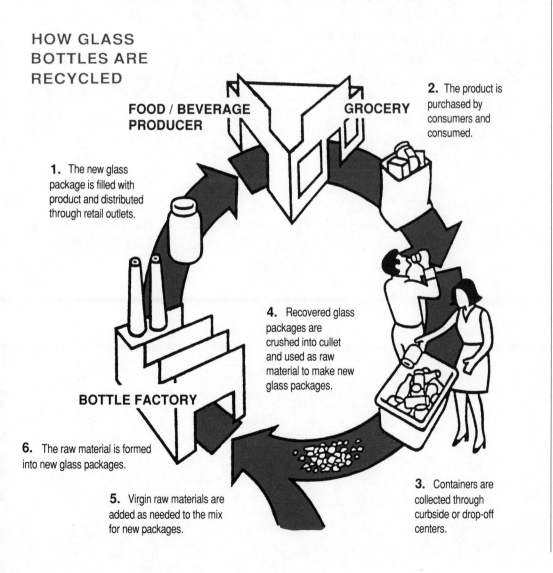

FOOD / BEVERAGE PRODUCER

GROCERY

2. The product is purchased by consumers and consumed.

1. The new glass package is filled with product and distributed through retail outlets.

4. Recovered glass packages are crushed into cullet and used as raw material to make new glass packages.

BOTTLE FACTORY

6. The raw material is formed into new glass packages.

5. Virgin raw materials are added as needed to the mix for new packages.

3. Containers are collected through curbside or drop-off centers.

6. *Recycle* glass containers so that they can be made into new glass bottles and jars.

———

Recycling means giving a boost to the economy and to the environment.

Recycling means closing landfills before they close in on us.

Recycling means cutting energy use.

Recycling means creating a new industry with lots of new jobs. (Some people have found jobs that might otherwise not be available to them. New York, for example, trains mentally retarded persons to work in recycling centers as glass sorters and separators. Wearing protective gear for their eyes and their hands, they stand alongside a conveyer belt carrying waste glass and separate the material by color and content. The work gives them an opportunity to make friends, develop self-esteem and independence, and earn an income.)

Most of all, recycling gives everyone a chance to be part of the effort to save the planet we all share.

———

P.S. Recycling can also mean letting your creativity loose. Use your imagination to turn glass discards into something new, something beautiful, and something useful. The following section on crafts will show you how creative recycling can help you make some very exciting things.

CRAFT IT !

Keep a Recycling Treasure Chest

You can be creative and, at the same time, be a friend to the environment by reusing glass in your craft projects. Most of the materials that you will need can be found at home. Collect jars and bottles of various sizes, shapes, and colors; save used light bulbs, mirrors, picture glass, and other glass objects.

Instead of throwing out greeting cards, wrapping paper, ribbons, bits of cloth, holiday decorations, yarn, and artificial flowers, save them in a recycling treasure chest. Use a shoe box for smaller items and a large corrugated carton to hold everything else.

However, you may need to purchase some tools and special materials to supplement your supplies. These items are not expensive and are generally available at local craft, hobby, art supply, variety, and discount stores.

Since you probably have a pencil, paper, ruler, and scissors on hand, these will not be listed under the Materials Section in the instructions. Some supplies you may need are brushes, paints, colored felt-tip pens or markers, felt, tracing paper, graphite or carbon paper, eraser, straight pins, masking tape, cardboard, paper towels, newspapers, round toothpicks, waxpaper, tacky glue, white craft glue, craft stick, and window cleaner.

Others will be mentioned at the beginning of each project.

General Instructions

Be sure to read all the instructions for the project you plan to do before you begin. Make sure that you wash your glass bottles, jars, and lids, removing labels and glue residue. Dry them well. Wipe mirrors and

27

plate-glass objects with window cleaner and paper towels before beginning your project. If you are not using a lid in your project and your object has one, tuck it away and save it for another future recycling idea. Cover your working area with newspaper to protect the table surface.

To transfer a pattern from the book, place tracing paper over the pattern and trace it with a pencil. On your workspace, lay a piece of cardboard larger than the pattern. Place graphite (or carbon) transfer paper, graphite side down, on the cardboard. (If you don't have any graphite paper, you can make your own by using the side of a pencil tip to stroke heavily and evenly back and forth over the entire side of a piece of white paper.) Lay the traced pattern on top of the graphite paper and trace the pattern with your pencil. Remove the pattern and graphite paper. Cut out the cardboard pattern and you are ready to trace your design.

To use a cardboard pattern, lay the pattern on top of the material called for in your project and trace around the pattern with a pencil. Then cut on the penciled lines.

To use a paper pattern, pin the paper pattern to the fabric and cut out around the pattern.

Here's a gluing tip: Use a craft stick to transfer glue from the jar to a piece of waxed paper. Apply glue to large surfaces with the craft stick and to small surfaces with a round toothpick; or you can spread the glue with your finger. A glue gun may be used to apply pom-poms and bows to any surface. A low-temperature glue gun and glue sticks may be used safely without adult supervision, but if you have a hot-glue gun, ask an adult to help you.

Whenever you work with glass, you should be very careful so you do not cut yourself. Handle light bulbs and the like very gently. When working with glass panes, picture glass, and mirrors, adult supervision is necessary.

If you use the materials suggested in the project instructions, your results should look very similar to the drawings. However, using found materials and lots of imagination will provide you with delightful original creations, ideal for your own use and for gifts.

GLASS RECYCLING IDEAS

Type	Uses
1. JARS Mayonnaise, pickle, apple or tomato sauce, peanut butter, baby food, pimento, olive, cherry, cold cream, make-up	**Large:** doorstops, vases **Medium:** potpourri, vases, pencil holders **Small:** mixing and storing paints; storing pins, paper clips; seed starters; votive candle holders **All:** paint or etch; storage for desktop, kitchen, or nursery; dolls; party favors, paperweights; assemblages; colored-sand art; decoupage; coin banks; gift containers; terrariums
2. BOTTLES Catsup, vegetable oil, salad dressing, soda, wine, liquor, nail polish	Bud vase, candlestick, table centerpieces, lamp bases, dolls, assemblages, doorstops
3. LIGHT BULBS Standard (white and colored), night-lights, Christmas tree, chandelier (flame-shaped)	Party-favor animals, potpourri sachet, base for papier-mâché, Christmas tree or window ornaments, heads for decorations or dolls
4. DRINKING GLASSES Water, juice, stemware	Hand paint or etch; vases, candle holders

5. DECORATIVE AND FUNCTIONAL GLASS

Vase	Lamp base
Fish bowl	Terrarium
Mirrors	Wall hangings, Christmas tree ornaments
Window or picture pane	Paint or etch; window or wall hangings, plant base
Watch or chandelier crystal	Jewelry, Christmas tree or window decoration
Beads, buttons	Jewelry, dollhouse decor, doll clothes trim, game counters, assemblages, animal eyes
Marbles	Store in a jar as a paperweight, in a vase as a lower arranger; animals
Eyeglasses	Pendants, pins, Christmas tree or window ornaments
Magnifying lens	Paperweight, Christmas tree or window ornaments
Broken glass (use thick pieces; handle with care, under adult supervision!)	Mosaics, collages

LIGHT BULB SACHET

All you need is an old light bulb, some glue, lace, netting, potpourri, ribbons, and flowers to create a lovely sachet to hang in a closet, bath, bedroom, kitchen or to tuck into a drawer. Make one for yourself and then make some more, and give one to your mom, sister, grandma, aunt, teacher, or friends. It's easy—just follow each step and the diagrams, too.

MATERIALS
- Used light bulb
- One 1' square piece of lace
- Two 1' square pieces of colored tulle netting
- One 1' square piece of tulle netting, of another color
- 4 yds 1/16" wide satin ribbon
- Six small artificial or dried flowers
- 1 cup potpourri (a mixture of fragrant, dried flowers, herbs, and spices, which can be purchased at craft or gift shops and department stores)
- Tacky glue
- Glue gun (low-temperature glue gun is best) and glue sticks
- Paper towels
- 12" round dinner plate
- 9" round salad plate
- Posterboard or cardboard
- Pen
- Potpourri oil (optional)

INSTRUCTIONS

1. Spread out four paper towels on a flat surface, leaving them connected.

2. Beginning at rounded end of light bulb, generously smear tacky glue on entire surface of bulb including screw base. Set aside.

3. Pour potpourri on one end of paper towels. Roll and press the light bulb in the potpourri until the bulb is completely covered. Glue dries clear, so don't worry if some of it shows. Set aside.

4. Place 12" dinner plate on cardboard and draw around edge of plate. Cut out cardboard circle. Repeat, using the 9" plate.

5. Place 12" cardboard circle on lace. Using pen, trace around circle and cut out one piece (a). Place 9" circle on tulle netting. Trace and then cut out two circles of one color (b) and one circle of the other color (c). Trim off any ink marks.

6. Place a tulle circle of each color (b) and (c) on top of lace circle (a) and set aside.

7. Cut two 1 yd length ribbons.

8. Place the remaining 9" tulle circle over screw base of light bulb (d). Tie each ribbon around narrow end (e). Knot ends of ribbon together to make a loop for hanging the finished sachet. Turn edges of tulle up over ribbon and screw base (f).

9. Now place light bulb in center of three layers (one lace, two tulle) and gather layers around bulb tightly.

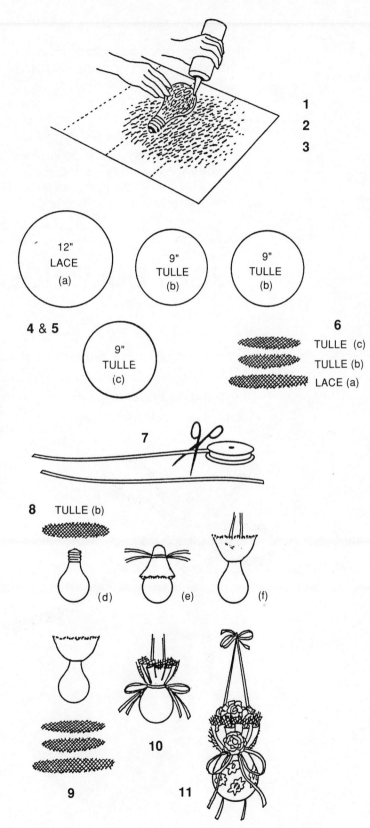

10. Cut two more 1 yd ribbons. Tie each around gathered lace at screw base. Tie bows on each side and let streamers hang down.

11. Using glue gun (or tacky glue), glue flowers on top of bow and screw base.

12. To make the fragrance stronger or to renew it, add a few drops of potpourri oil at the neck of the light bulb. Hang the sachet in your closet and enjoy!

VARIATIONS

Precut lace and tulle circles are available at craft stores. If they are used, omit steps 4 and 5.

If you don't have lace and tulle, you can experiment with substitutions of other lightweight fabrics and trim you have at home.

LIGHT BULB HOLIDAY ORNAMENTS

Brush some glittery gold paint on a used light bulb; then add a bow and a few holly leaves to create a simple holiday tree or window ornament. Or paint and decorate several, in any way you wish, to make your own one-of-a-kind ornaments.

MATERIALS
- Used light bulb(s) (standard size or smaller)
- Gold metallic paint or other colors, as desired
- Liquid glitter paint
- Paintbrush
- Scrap of red and green satin ribbon
- 1/4 yd red satin ribbon
- 6" length thin wire
- Tacky glue
- Gold braid or other cord or ribbon
- Optional trim, such as holly leaves (can be made from felt) and sequins

INSTRUCTIONS

1. Paint light bulb with two coats gold paint. Allow it to dry well between coats.

2. When bulb is dry, paint with one coat liquid glitter paint. Let dry well.

3. Twist wire around end of light bulb, forming loop. Snip off excess wire.

4. Glue scrap of red ribbon around end of light bulb, then glue green ribbon next to it.

5. Tie 1/4 yd of red ribbon around light bulb and tie bow. Add desired trim to bow.

6. Tie cord through wire loop to hang ornament.

1 & 2

VARIATIONS

It's easy to imagine turning light bulbs into a variety of items. How many can you think of? Here are a few to get you started.

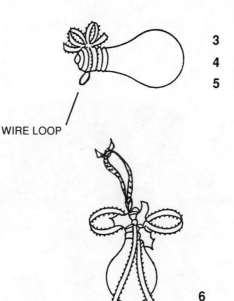

3
4
5

WIRE LOOP

6

When making papier-mâché animals, you can create interesting heads by covering light bulbs with some of the papier-mâché. Or spray-paint amusing bulb-heads. Use the techniques for adding elements and decorations that you'll find in the following projects of this book. Your imagination is the only limit.

33

SUPER SIMPLE JAR TOPPERS

Any size jar can become a decorative container to store candy, snacks, or your collectibles when you top it off with a flat or puffy jar topper. For gifts, you may want to use fabric scraps that you have on hand. For yourself, why not make toppers from fabric scraps that match your home decor?

MATERIALS

- Any size jar with screw-top lid
- Fabric scraps
- Rubber band
- Polyfill or cotton balls
- Thick tacky glue
- Needle
- Quilting thread
- Pinking shears
- Saucer or plate
- Iron

INSTRUCTIONS

1. Unscrew lid from jar. Wash and dry jar and lid well. Be sure jar is free from any glue residue.
2. Press fabric scraps with iron.

For Flat-top Lid

3. With ruler, measure diameter (width) of lid. Cut out a square of fabric with sides double that measurement.
4. Use a saucer or plate approximately the same size as the cut fabric and trace around it on the wrong (back) side of fabric square .
5. Cut out circle with pinking shears. (If you don't use pinking shears, the fabric may fray.)

6. Lay fabric circle on top of lid and place rubber band around top of lid over fabric circle.

7. With pinking shears, cut strip of fabric 1/2" x 18" long. Tie strip around jar lid, covering rubber band. Tie a shoestring bow.

For Puff-top Lid

8. With ruler, measure diameter of lid. Cut out a square of fabric with sides triple that measurement.

9. Use a saucer or plate approximately the same size as the cut fabric and trace around the plate on the wrong side of the fabric square.

10. Cut out circle with pinking shears.

11. Thread needle and knot end of thread. With right (front) side of fabric facing you, stitch around edge of circle 1" in from edge.

12. Pull ends of thread together to gather fabric circle slightly.

13. Place a large handful of polyfill or cotton balls in center of the wrong side of the gathered circle and continue to draw in threads, adding more filling as you tighten circle. Lay stuffed circle aside.

14. Smear glue on middle portion of rim of lid and on top of lid.

15. Place gathered edge of stuffed circle over glued rim, and draw threads tightly, tying them into a double knot. Cut off ends.

16. Adjust gathers of fabric, so puffy top appears even. Screw lid on jar. Adjust gathers again, if necessary.

Fill jars with candy, your favorite treats, or collectibles. Tall jars are great for spaghetti or other pasta. A puff top makes a handy pin cushion for a jar filled with buttons.

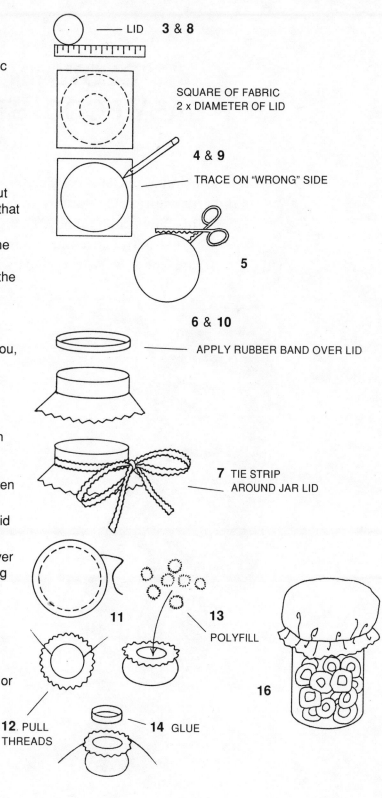

LID **3 & 8**

SQUARE OF FABRIC
2 x DIAMETER OF LID

4 & 9

TRACE ON "WRONG" SIDE

5

6 & 10

APPLY RUBBER BAND OVER LID

7 TIE STRIP
AROUND JAR LID

11

13
POLYFILL

16

12. PULL THREADS

14 GLUE

"CLOWNIN' AROUND"
BABY FOOD STORAGE JARS

Tell mom not to toss out baby sister's or brother's baby food jars! They make great storage containers for school items, such as rubber bands, paper clips, and lunch money. Using felt, paint, and glue, follow these easy instructions to start your own clownin' around now; before you know it, your friends will be clownin' around, too.

CLOWN SITTERS

MATERIALS

- Baby food jar(s), 2.8 oz size
- One each of 9" x 12" felt pieces of neon colors (pink, yellow, green, and orange)
- One each of 9" x 12" felt pieces of black and white
- One skein red 4-ply sport yarn (or two 2-ply skeins)
- One 31.8 mm (about 1") or 36.5 mm (about 1 1/2") wooden bead for the head
- Thick tacky glue
- Clear acrylic spray
- Black and white acrylic paint
- Small paintbrush
- Tracing paper
- Pinking shears (optional)
- Round toothpick
- Pen or pencil
- Straight pins
- Felt-tip pens (black, red, and orange)
- Paper towels
- Medium pom-poms (about 1/2")

INSTRUCTIONS

Preparation

1. Wash jar(s) and lid(s). Dry well.

2. Place tracing paper on patterns on following pages. Trace and cut out all patterns. (See General Instructions, p. 27.)

3. Select the colored felt you plan to use for each clown jar. For example, you may want one clown to be dressed in orange and yellow; another, in pink and green. Use black and white felt for mitts and boots: black with white trim or vice versa.

4. Lay patterns on felt. Pin patterns in place. Cut out all pieces and do not remove pinned patterns. Set aside. You will remove pins and patterns when you get ready to assemble each clown jar.

Making Clown Face

5. For clown head, paint wooden bead with two coats of white paint. Dry well between coats. Follow the next steps for placement of face parts, as shown. Let dry well between each step.

6. Dip end of small paint brush in black paint. Then dab end of brush on paper towel to remove excess paint. To make eyes, place dots on painted wooden bead as shown.

7. Add eyelid to bottom of each eye dot with black felt-tip pen.

8. Add eyebrows over eye dots with black pen.

9. Mark nose under and between eye dots with red felt-tip pen.

10. Paint red "hot dog"-shaped mouth under nose.

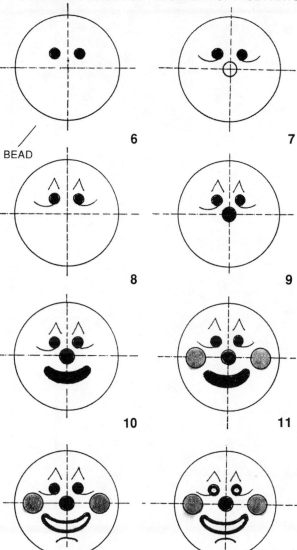

DO NOT DRAW CROSSED LINES ON FACE. THEY ARE A GUIDE FOR PLACEMENT OF FACE PARTS.

BEAD

6   7   8   9   10   11   12.   13. & 14.

11. Make orange circles at end of mouth for cheeks.

12. Paint small white "hot dog" smile over red mouth after it is dry. Mark chin with black pen.

13. Dip end of small paintbrush into white paint and add dots to corner of eyes.

PATTERNS

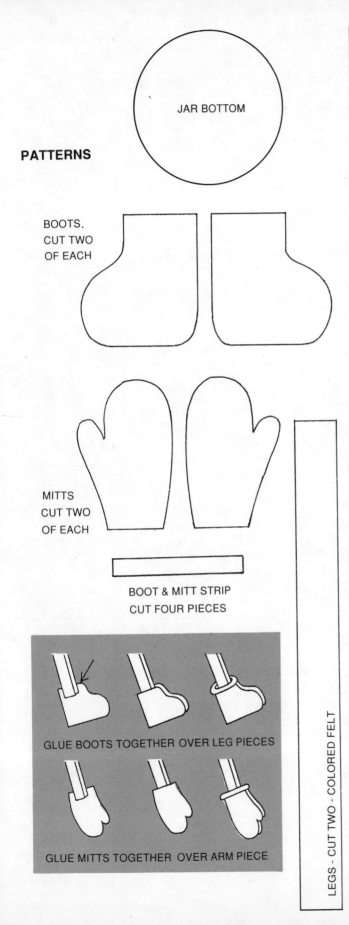

JAR BOTTOM

BOOTS.
CUT TWO
OF EACH

MITTS
CUT TWO
OF EACH

BOOT & MITT STRIP
CUT FOUR PIECES

GLUE BOOTS TOGETHER OVER LEG PIECES

GLUE MITTS TOGETHER OVER ARM PIECE

LEGS - CUT TWO - COLORED FELT

ARMS - CUT ONE - COLORED FELT

ASSEMBLY

14. Dip round toothpick into black paint and add black dots over white dots. Let face dry thoroughly overnight.

15. Next day spray with clear acrylic. Set aside and work on clown's body.

Assembling Clown

Remember—unpin the pieces as you assemble clown. Tip: When gluing felt on glass, always smear glue on glass with your finger, then press felt piece to glass object firmly with fingers. (Do not smear glue onto felt—too messy!)

16. *Jar bottom.* Smear glue on bottom of jar. Press felt circle in place on jar bottom.

17. *Legs and boots.* Smear glue on one side of boot. Place end of leg over top edge of boot. Place a matching boot on top of end of leg and press together firmly. Repeat for second boot, pointing toe of boot in opposite direction. Take narrow strips of black or white felt (whichever wasn't used to

make boots). Glue around boot tops. Overlap and glue ends together. Glue tops of legs to bottom of jar (see finished clown, p. 36).

18. *Arms and mitts.* Smear glue on one side of mitt. Place end of arm over top edge of mitt. Place a matching mitt on top of end of arm and press together firmly. Repeat for second mitt, pointing thumb of mitt in opposite direction. Take narrow strips of black or white felt (whichever wasn't used to make mitt). Glue around mitt tops. Overlap and glue ends together.

19. *Arm placement.* Remove lid from jar. Smear glue at back of jar under "lip" of jar. Press middle of the arms' strip of felt on glued area and bring the arms forward, gluing in place.

20. *Body.* Glue body felt strip to lower 1/3 portion of jar. Glue belt in place. For buckle, cut 1" square of black felt and fold in half. Cut out small square in center of fold. Cut square around hole. Glue belt buckle in center of belt.

21. *Collar.* Glue collar felt strip to outer rim of jar lid, overlapping and gluing edges down. Glue large felt circle to top of jar lid and small circle on top of that. Screw lid onto jar.

22. *Hair.* Cut 2 yd length of yarn for each clown head. Pull each ply of yarn apart and gather together into a knotted-looking mess. Smear glue onto back, sides, and top of clown head. Press hair onto glue and "mold" hair around head. (Note: if adding hat to clown head, glue hat on first; put glue around sides and back of clown head and press yarn hair in place.) Glue clown head on top of felt circles on lid.

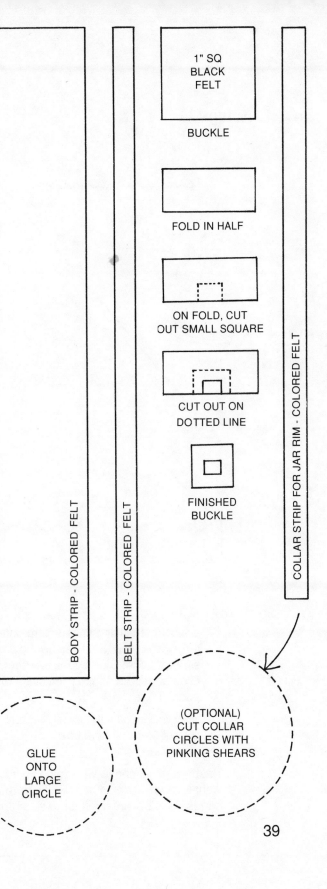

1" SQ BLACK FELT

BUCKLE

FOLD IN HALF

ON FOLD, CUT OUT SMALL SQUARE

CUT OUT ON DOTTED LINE

FINISHED BUCKLE

BODY STRIP - COLORED FELT

BELT STRIP - COLORED FELT

COLLAR STRIP FOR JAR RIM - COLORED FELT

GLUE ONTO LARGE CIRCLE

(OPTIONAL) CUT COLLAR CIRCLES WITH PINKING SHEARS

39

CLOWN HAT PATTERN

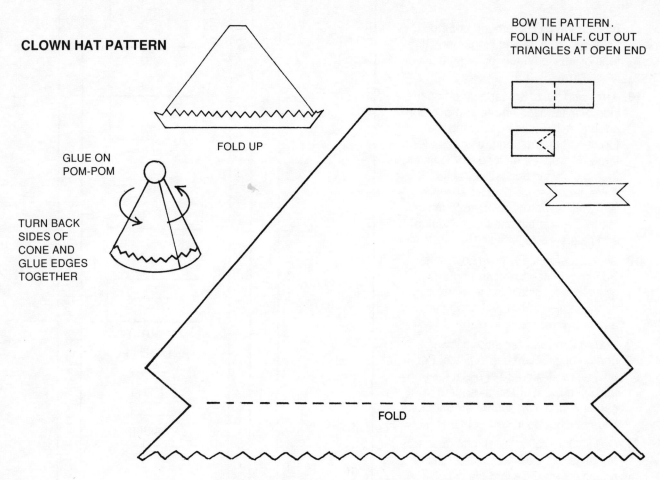

FOLD UP

GLUE ON
POM-POM

TURN BACK
SIDES OF
CONE AND
GLUE EDGES
TOGETHER

FOLD

CUT THIS EDGE ONLY WITH PINKING SHEARS (OPTIONAL)

23. *Hat.* Optional for 36.5 mm bead. With scissors or pinking shears, trim bottom edge of felt flap. Fold flap up. Fold back sides of cone. Glue edges together. Glue pom-pom or small felt circle to peak of hat.

24. *Bow tie.* For bow tie, fold felt in half and cut out triangle. Glue bow tie under clown head chin.

Unscrew jar lid and fill with anything you want to store, such as paper clips or rubber bands. This is a great gift for desk or shelf.

VARIATIONS

Instead of using wooden beads for heads, you may wish to experiment with various balls, such as Ping-Pong, rubber, golf, plastic foam.

To decorate larger jar, you may want to use larger bead head or plastic foam ball for clown head. You can even make arms and legs longer, if you wish. Also, you can use scraps of heavy fabric instead of felt. Make a different funny hat for each jar. Just remember—have fun—"clownin' around!"

40

CLOWN HEAD JAR

MATERIALS

- Baby food jar 4 oz size
- One skein 4-ply red (or other bright color) sport yarn (or two 2-ply skeins)
- Thick tacky glue
- Tracing paper
- Pinking sheers (optional)
- One each of 9" x 12" felt pieces of orange and two other neon colors, such as green, yellow, or pink
- One each of 9" x 12" felt pieces of black, white, and red
- One medium red pom-pom (about 1/2")
- Straight pins

INSTRUCTIONS

1. Trace and cut out patterns for lid and face pieces. (See General Instructions, p. 27.)

IF THIS LID PATTERN DOES NOT FIT YOUR JAR, TRACE AND CUT PATTERN FROM YOUR OWN LID

MOUTH (RED)

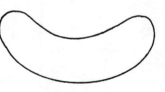

GRIN (WHITE)

EYEBROWS (BLACK)

EYES (BLACK)

INSIDE EYES

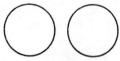

CHEEKS (ORANGE)

BOW TIE (BLACK)

FOLD

SNIP

TIE

NOSE (RED FELT OR POM-POM)

2. Pin patterns to colored felt selected for each face piece. Cut them out.

3. Cut yarn into ten 1 yd lengths. Pull plies (strands) apart on all cut lengths.

4. Place large dab of glue on fingers. Dampen under faucet and knead (squeeze) all yarn lengths together until they look like a knotted mess. Set aside. Wash hands.

5. Spread glue on top of jar lid.

6. Press felt circle for lid firmly in place.

7. Smear glue on top of felt lid circle.

8. Cut a small bunch of the glued yarn from the ball you made and press and spread on top of jar lid till felt circle is covered. Be sure to glue and press yarn mess around lid rim, too.

9. Glue felt face pieces in place.

10. Glue smaller (inner) collar on top of larger (outer) collar. Then glue it onto base of jar. For bow tie, fold black felt lengthwise. Cut out triangles from each end. Tie thread of yarn around center of tie to pinch it in.

11. Smear glue on sides, top and back of jar.

12. Spread out remaining glued yarn mess and press into glue, shaping hairline. Tip: wait till lid and jar dry well before replacing lid on jar.

This fun-to-make little container will store lunch money or the spending money you're saving for something special.

COLLAR PATTERNS

OUTER COLLAR
CUT WITH PINKING
SHEARS (OPTIONAL)

INNER COLLAR
CUT WITH PINKING
SHEARS (OPTIONAL)

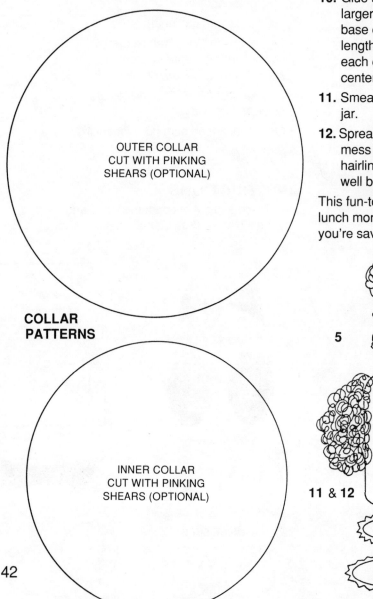

42

EASY-DO DECOUPAGE CONTAINERS

Don't toss them away! Save those bottles and jars and turn them into usable home decoration containers NOW! Ask mom for a few pretty paper guest napkins or hand towels, and surprise her with your own original creation for your home or for gift giving.

MATERIALS

- Any size bottle or jar
- Decorative 3-ply paper napkins or hand towels with floral, holiday, birthday, or other designs on white background
- Mod Podge
- White (preferably, snow white) acrylic paint
- Paintbrush
- Fine sandpaper
- One 6" x 6" piece of white felt
- 1/2 yd double-faced satin ribbon
- Tacky glue
- Optional decorations—greens (ivy, holly), candle, matching napkins or handtowels

INSTRUCTIONS

1. Remove label and wash bottle or jar. Dry well.
2. Paint bottle or jar with two coats white acrylic paint. Allow to dry between coats of paint. Wash paintbrush well.
3. Cut designs from 3-ply napkins, leaving space around edge of design.

4. Brush one coat Mod Podge over entire painted surface to protect paint from chipping.

5. Decide how you want to place designs on bottle or jar.

6. Brush thin coat of Mod Podge on small area of glass. Separate plies from design, and using top ply only, place design over Mod Podge. Smooth out any air bubbles with brush. (Dispose of other two plies.)

7. Continue brushing on Mod Podge and add top ply of each design to different places on bottle or jar.

8. After all designs are glued into place with Mod Podge, brush one coat of Mod Podge over entire glass surface. Dry well.

9. Brush five or six coats of Mod Podge over entire glass surface, allowing it to dry well (one hour) between coats. The more coats you brush on, the more Mod Podge will build up and give depth to your designs. (Note: if, after brushing on three coats of Mod Podge, you feel any rough spots, you can sand lightly with fine sandpaper).

10. Trace bottom of container onto felt. Cut out and glue to bottom of decoupaged container to protect surface of table.

11. Tie ribbon around neck of bottle or jar and tie shoestring bow, if desired.

If you decorate a wide-mouthed jar, you may use it to hold matching or plain napkins, which looks pretty on a party table. Or you may fill it with greens, flowers, or candy. A small-mouthed bottle could hold a candle or a flower or two. Or use your own ideas to fashion unique containers.

WIDE-MOUTHED JAR

VARIATIONS

You can experiment using other paper cut-outs; but if you use heavier paper, as from a magazine, you will need to use more coats of Mod Podge to blend in the picture. Pictures with white backgrounds work best. For example, you may select a magazine picture of a horse's head. Draw a circle around it and cut out. Follow the above directions, using extra coats of Mod Podge. You may then glue a gold braid (or cord) around the circle to frame the horse's portrait. Tie another gold braid around the mouth of the jar.

CUT THREE PLIES OF NAPKIN. USE TOP PLY ONLY.

3.

6.

8. & 9.

10.

MIRROR, MIRROR ON THE WALL

Just scout around the house and you're sure to find an old odd-shaped mirror or two tucked away in mom's pocketbook or "catch-all" drawer. Don't toss them out. Create these clever wall hangings to decorate a bare spot, or to hang along with your favorite photos or pictures.

MATERIALS

- Mirrors (any size or shape)
- Scrap piece of felt large enough to "back" mirror
- Scrap of lace long enough to fit around edge of mirror
- 1/2 to 1 yd of ribbon, any width of 1" or more (narrower for small mirror)
- Thick tacky glue
- Hot-glue gun (with adult supervision only) or low-temperature glue gun and glue sticks
- Pen
- "D" ring or round brass curtain ring

45

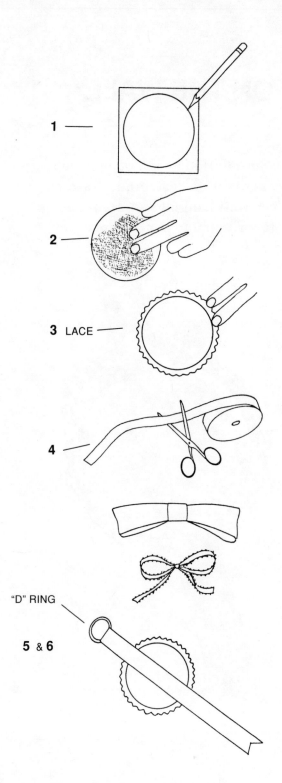

1 —

2 —

3 LACE —

4 —

"D" RING —

5 & 6

INSTRUCTIONS

1. Lay mirror face down on piece of felt. Trace perimeter (outline) of mirror with pen or pencil. Cut out felt shape.

2. Smear tacky glue with finger on back of mirror. Press felt in place.

3. With glue gun, run "worm" or bead of glue around back edge of mirror (on top of felt) and press lace around edge, overlapping ends at top of mirror.

4. Cut 10" length of ribbon and tie shoestring or tailored style bow. Glue to top of mirror.

5. Cut length of ribbon to use for backing. Glue it across center of back of mirror with about 4" extending from top.

6. Slip top of ribbon through "D" ring. Fold back ribbon and glue down. Hang on wall alone or with a group of photos or pictures to create a unique wall decor.

For small mirror, fold 1/2 yd of narrow ribbon in half and tie loop for hanger. Glue securely to back of mirror. Tie shoestring bow and glue over lace edging at top of mirror.

VARIATIONS

There are many different mirror designs that you can try. Vary your materials. Sew or glue on buttons or artificial flowers or add pins or anything else your imagination conjures up. These items make wonderful gifts for all occasions.

WINTER WONDERFUL SNOWMAN

For the holidays or until spring arrives, this fun little fella will add a cheery note to help chase away those winter "blahs." Using a squatty-type jar, light bulb, felt and pom-poms, you can whip him up in just a few hours' time. Stuff him with cotton balls or fiberfill stuffing for the true snowy(man's) look!

MATERIALS

- One squatty-shaped jar
- One used light bulb
- 9" x 12" piece of black felt
- Scraps of red and orange felt
- Three small black pom-poms (about 3/8")
- Seven mini black pom-poms (about 1/8")
- White acrylic paint
- Clear acrylic sealer
- Paintbrush
- Cotton balls or fiberfill batting
- Thick tacky glue
- Pen or pencil
- Scrap cardboard
- Tracing paper
- Graphite (or carbon) paper
- Small feather (optional)

INSTRUCTIONS

1. Wash jar, removing label and glue residue. Dry well. Set jar aside.
2. Paint light bulb with two coats white acrylic paint. Let dry well between coats.

PATTERNS

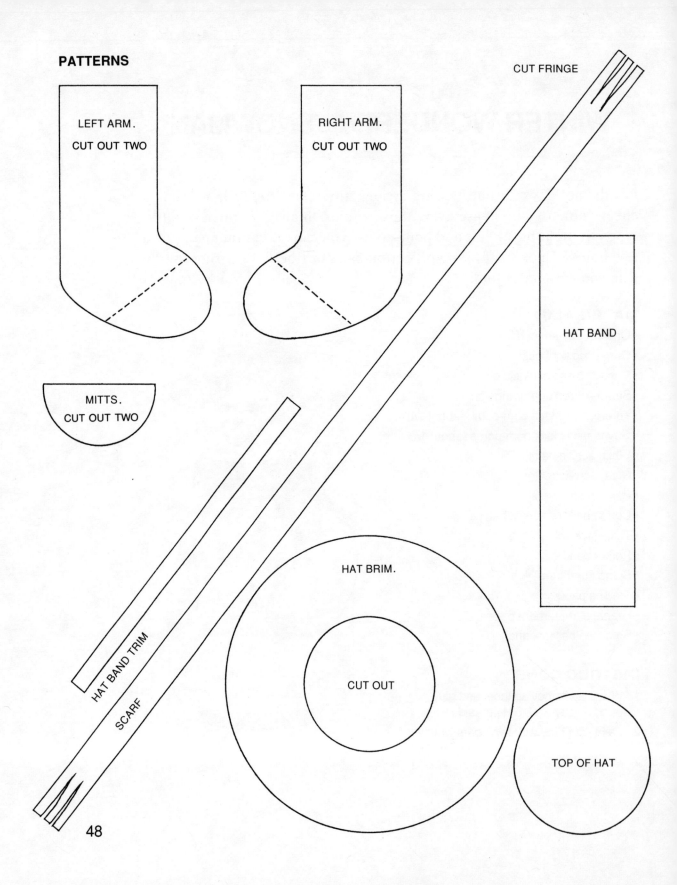

LEFT ARM.
CUT OUT TWO

RIGHT ARM.
CUT OUT TWO

CUT FRINGE

MITTS.
CUT OUT TWO

HAT BAND

HAT BAND TRIM

SCARF

HAT BRIM.

CUT OUT

TOP OF HAT

48

3. Paint or spray on clear varnish sealer. Dry well.

4. Make all of the patterns for the snowman's arms, mitts, scarf, hat, and nose; and cut them out of felt. (See General Instructions, p. 27, on how to make cardboard patterns.)

5. Glue together the two right arm pieces, then two left arm pieces. Glue each arm onto jar.

6. Glue black mitts on end of each arm.

7. Fill jar with cotton balls or fiberfill, creating hole in center. Place painted light bulb in center of hole. Do not glue in place.

8. Assemble hat. Glue ends of hat band (crown) together, forming tube. Glue edges of hat brim to crown. Glue hat band trim around seam. (If glue shows, dab with black acrylic paint to hide.)

9. Glue mini black pom-poms in place for eyes and mouth.

10. Fashion "carrot" nose by gluing long sides together.

11. Tie red felt scarf around neck and glue in place. Cut ends of scarf to make fringe.

12. Glue three small pom-pom "coal" buttons down the front of the jar.

13. Spread glue on inside rim of hat and position it on head. Glue small feather on outer rim of hat, if desired.

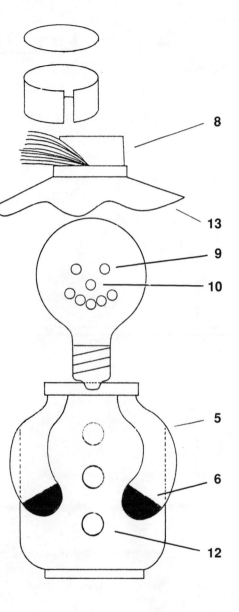

CARROT NOSE PATTERN

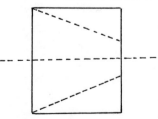

CUT FROM ORANGE FELT GLUE LONG SIDES TOGETHER

49

HOLIDAY TREE JAR

Using felt strips and pom-poms, you can create a one-of-a-kind table-top tree. Fill the jar with colored green water, or paint the jar with green paint, if you like. Add natural or artificial greens to the top to make this very special decoration. Why not make several, and grow your own forest? Or set a Winter Wonderful Snowman next to your tree to create a winter scene.

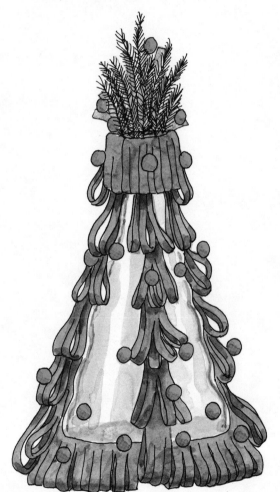

MATERIALS

- 8" salad dressing jar
- Green food or egg dye
- 1 cup water
- 9" x 12" piece of green felt
- Twelve each red, yellow, white, or other colored medium (about 1/2") pom-poms (or colored beads or pearls)
- Sprig of natural or artificial greens
- Candle (optional)
- Thick tacky glue

INSTRUCTIONS

1. Wash jar, removing label and glue residue. Dry well. (Put lid in your treasure chest for future use.)
2. Cut twenty-two 4" x 1/2" strips of green felt for long loops.

3. Cut twenty-six 2 1/2" x 1/2" strips of green felt for short loops.

4. Glue ends of all felt pieces together to form loops.

5. Cut through all glued felt loop pieces in thirds, as shown.

6. Beginning at the bottom sides of jar, glue flat ends of six of the long loops to each side of jar up to neck of bottle.

7. Next, glue five long loops to center of both front and back of jar.

8. Around jar bottom, glue four short loops in between each set of the longer loops, slightly overhanging the edge. At each side, tuck one more short loop under the long loops to cover bottom edge completely.

9. Glue eight short loops around top of jar.

10. To trim tree, glue pom-poms or beads on glass and loops, as you wish.

11. Fill measuring cup with tap water. Add three drops of green food coloring and stir well. Pour carefully into jar.

12. Cut sprig of greens and tuck in top of jar. Glue on more pom-poms. For a narrow top jar, skip the greens and add a candle.

Set jar on table—and enjoy!

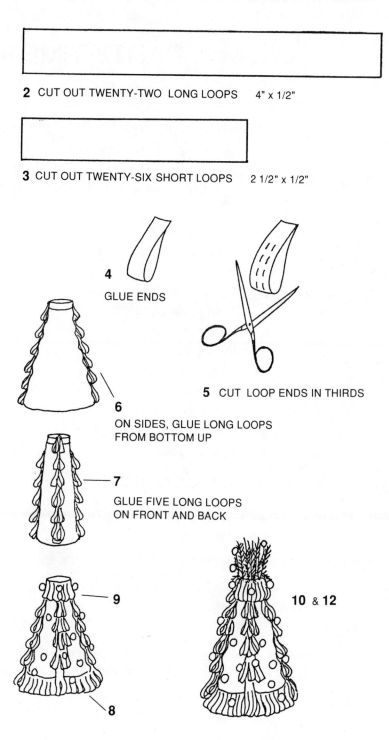

2 CUT OUT TWENTY-TWO LONG LOOPS   4" x 1/2"

3 CUT OUT TWENTY-SIX SHORT LOOPS   2 1/2" x 1/2"

4 GLUE ENDS

5 CUT LOOP ENDS IN THIRDS

6 ON SIDES, GLUE LONG LOOPS FROM BOTTOM UP

7 GLUE FIVE LONG LOOPS ON FRONT AND BACK

9

8

10 & 12

PARTY TIME ILLUMINARIES

Save those mayonnaise jars, both large and small, and create an elegant decor for party time or anytime. With sugar, paint, glue, and glitter, you can create these very special illuminaries, or votives, for yourself or for a gift for those you hold near and dear.

MATERIALS

- Large or small mayonnaise jar(s)
- 1 cup white sugar
- 1/2 cup gold or silver glitter
- White acrylic paint
- Thick tacky glue
- White votive candle
- Scrap of white felt
- 1/2 yd gold cord or ribbon (for each jar)
- Pen or pencil
- Small dish and spoon
- Measuring cup

INSTRUCTIONS

1. Wash jar(s), removing label and glue residue. Wash lid. Dry both well. Set lid aside.

2. Measure 1 cup sugar and pour into dish. Measure 1/2 cup glitter and pour on top of sugar. Stir together well.

3. Run fingers under water faucet and flick several drops of water into jar. Turn on side, rotating jar in your hands to distribute water droplets.

4. Place 1 teaspoon sugar and glitter mixture in jar and rotate jar, distributing mixture over water droplets. Mixture will cling to sides willy-nilly. (Note: if you have added too much water, and your jar is too heavily coated with sugar mixture, simply rinse out jar, dry well, and start over.) Allow jar to dry for several hours or overnight.

5. Dampen sides of candle with fingers, roll candle in mixture. Allow to dry.

To Decorate Lid

6. Turn lid over and place top side face down on felt. Trace with pen or pencil and cut out.

7. Smear glue on top of lid and press felt circle into place. Press down with fingers at edges. Set aside to dry.

8. Using a finger, smear mixture on outside rim of lid. Sprinkle on glitter. Allow to dry.

9. Place 1 tablespoon of glue in dish. Add 1 teaspoon white paint. Stir together well.

To Assemble Jar

10. Smear mixture on inside, outside, and top rim of jar.

11. Pour remaining sugar-glitter mixture into jar.

12. Place candle in center of mixture.

13. Tie cord or ribbon around top of jar and tie a shoestring bow.

Now place your illuminary on tabletop, windowsill, or mantle. At holiday or party time, why not make several to add a charming glow to a front porch or walk as guests arrive at your home?

FLICK DROPS OF
WATER INTO JAR AND ROTATE.
PLACE 1 TSP. SUGAR GLITTER
MIXTURE IN JAR AND ROTATE.

FELT

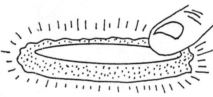

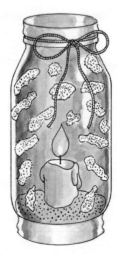

SET JAR ON LID

53

PAINTED PANE PICTURE

Create your own special modern abstract painting using a toss-away pane of glass, acrylic paint, the eraser end of a pencil, and plenty of imagination. You'll be surprised and delighted with the results.

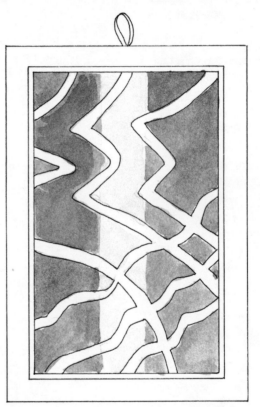

MATERIALS

- Any size glass pane or piece of glass
- A frame to fit, ready for hanging
- Acrylic paints (a must—other type paint may not produce results described in project)
- Wide and narrow paintbrushes
- Pencil with a good eraser
- Glossy clear liquid varnish (not spray)
- Paper towels
- Any size drawing paper
- Colored pencils or crayons
- Glass cleaner
- Thick tacky glue or low-temperature glue gun and glue sticks

INSTRUCTIONS

Whenever you use glass panes or picture glass, it is important to have adult supervision.

1. Wash and clean glass pane with cleaner. Dry well.

2. For pattern, lay glass pane on paper and trace around edges with pencil. Set pane aside.

3. Using colored pencils, divide pattern into three stripes.

4. Color in pattern lightly with pencil colors of your choice.

5. Now decide size of lines, squiggles, or whatever you want, and create your own pattern. (Your design will differ from the one shown here, since you will be using your own creativity.)

6. Lay clean glass pane on two paper towels.

7. Wipe top of pane with dampened paper towel to moisten glass.

8. Now, look at your pattern. Load wide brush with one color and paint stripe. Repeat, painting two other stripes, making sure that edges of stripes touch each other. (Note: if you make a mistake at any point in your painting or you change your mind as to colors and shapes, you simply wash your pane clean, and begin again.)

9. Using the eraser end of your pencil, press into painted pane following the lines and shapes in your sketched pattern. Be sure to sketch lines from one edge of glass to other edge. (Note: if lines are unclear, go back and repeat with eraser again, clearing away paint.)

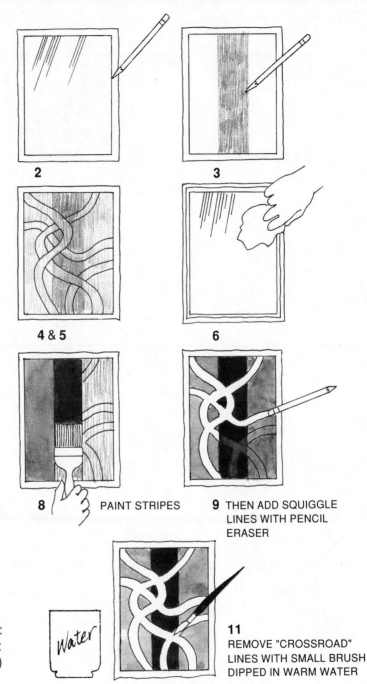

2

3

4 & 5

6

8 PAINT STRIPES

9 THEN ADD SQUIGGLE LINES WITH PENCIL ERASER

Water

11 REMOVE "CROSSROAD" LINES WITH SMALL BRUSH DIPPED IN WARM WATER

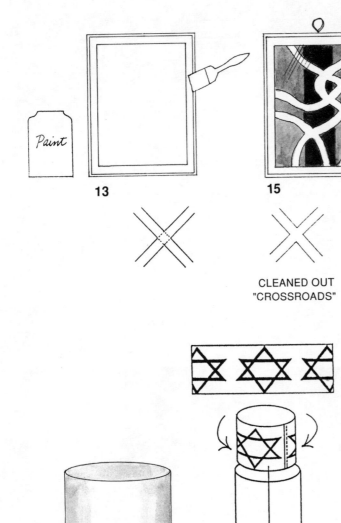

13

15

CLEANED OUT
"CROSSROADS"

10. Continue drawing design with eraser from edge to edge of glass, allowing paint colors to cross over each other as they merge. Allow design to dry ten minutes.

11. Dip small paintbrush in warm water and go over glass lines to smooth paint and clean out "crossroads" of paint. When all crossroads are free of paint, you are finished painting your design. Allow to dry one hour.

12. With small paintbrush, paint liquid varnish on painted portions of glass only. Allow to dry.

13. Paint frame, coordinating color if desired.

14. Place dab of glue in all four corners of inside of frame and press painted pane in place, painted side out.

15. Tie and glue on wire or ribbon loop to picture hanger on back of frame and hang in window or on wall.

VARIATIONS

You may glue on colored felt or fabric backing, if desired, and hang on wall.

The same techniques and materials may be used to make holiday or party glassware. Use a clean glass or jar. Moisten area to be painted with a damp towel. You may paint a freehand design on the glass. Or make a pattern on a piece of paper to fit inside the glass. Tape paper into a fixed position. With a paintbrush or tube of paint, draw outline of design on outside of glass, following pattern. Let dry. Then paint empty spaces with colors of your choice. Allow to dry thoroughly. Varnish. (Glass is for decorative use; don't put it in dishwasher.)

GLOSSARY

Bacteria. Single-celled microscopic organisms. Some can cause disease; others break down solid waste.

Buy-back Centers. Where people can take waste glass and are paid an agreed upon price when the material is accepted. The buy-back center sorts and packages the materials and sells them to the manufacturers for reprocessing. (Also see Recycler and Recycling Center.)

Contaminant. Material which, if not removed from waste glass, or cullet, can cause problems in the glassmaking process. Metal and pieces of paper are examples of contaminants.

Cullet. Pieces of waste glass used in the glassmaking process. This glass can come either from glass collected outside the glass factory or from the pieces broken during production.

Curbside Program. A program that provides a pick-up service for recyclable materials, which are collected on designated days and taken to recycling centers.

Degradable. Capable of decomposing.

Deposit. A fee (usually no more than five cents) paid at the time of purchase of a product packaged in a can, or a glass or plastic bottle. The fee is refunded when the empty container is returned. (Also see Redeem.)

Environment. Our surroundings: the air we breathe, the water we drink, and the land around us.

Environmental Protection Agency (EPA). The federal government office responsible for making our environment safe.

Fiberglass. Glass threads woven into yarns or pressed into sheets for use in boat hulls and car bodies; also used to make insulating materials.

Fiber Optics. The technology that uses light to carry communication signals over fine glass filaments wrapped in bundles. Each glass filament is as thin as a hair, and carries thousands of messages transmitted by pulses of light. Fiber optics is also used in lighted signs.

Glassphalt. Road material similar to asphalt; made with petroleum and cullet.

Glassmaker. A person or company that produces glass products.

Incinerator. A building where garbage and other waste materials are burned to create a smaller amount of solid waste in the form of ash.

Landfill. An area where solid waste is dumped and covered with soil.

Organism. Any living thing.

Pollution. Contamination of earth, water, or air from chemicals, gases, or solid wastes.

Recyclables. Almost anything made from natural materials and some man-made materials that can be reused. Most common recyclables include: paper, glass, aluminum, newspaper, cardboard, tin, motor oil, and plastics.

Recycler. (Or **Recycling Company.**) A business that purchases recyclables from organizations, municipalities, or individuals and resells the material for reprocessing. (Also see Buy-Back Center and Recycling Center.)

Recycling. Using waste materials to produce new materials.

Recycling Center. A place where materials for recycling are collected and then sent to a manufacturing plant. (Also see Buy-Back Center and Recycler.)

Redeem. To buy back the bottle or can on which a deposit has been paid. The store refunds a person's deposit when the container is returned.

Redemption Price. (Or **Redemption Fee.**) The price paid for recyclable materials. The buyer is usually a buy-back center or recycling center. The price varies depending on the area, quality, and color of the glass.

Reduce. To cut down on the source of waste materials. This can be done by (1) reusing materials to lower demand at the production level and (2) buying materials either in loose form (unpackaged) or with minimum packaging.

Reuse. To use an object or product again, either for its original purpose or for something new. For example, refilling a soda bottle with a beverage, or turning it into a vase.

Silicates. The most abundant naturally occurring substances on earth, made up of various types of rocks and minerals, such as calcium, quartz, talc, magnesium, and asbestos. Silicates are used in glass-making. Sand is the most common form of silicate.

Solid Waste. All garbage and trash, including household discards and industrial materials.

Glass Recycles

FIND OUT MORE

In theory almost everything can be recycled, but in practice a lot depends on you and your community. Listed here are the most common items that can be recovered and recycled before they go into the solid waste stream:

Paper. Newspaper, books, magazines, office papers, commercial print, corrugated packaging, folding cartons, cardboard, bags
Glass. Beer/soda bottles, wine/spirits bottles, food containers
Metal. Ferrous metal (iron and steel), including food and beverage cans, appliances, automobiles, aluminum, including so lead (car batteries), non-ferrous (such as copper and brass)
Plastic. Plates and cups, clothing and shoes, soft drink bottles, milk bottles, containers, bags, wraps
Rubber. Tires, clothing and shoes
Textiles and Leather. Clothing and shoes
Other Organic Material. Food, yard wastes, wood chips
Motor Oil.

Items not easily recyclable are oily rags, household batteries, paper mixed with food, disposable diapers, and other multi-material products that can't readily be separated into reusable materials.

A material is truly recyclable only if there is a recycling system in place. Successful recycling depends upon having the necessary technology to collect, sort, and process recoverable materials, as well as finding a market for them. Your community may be capable of providing programs for only a few of these items. To find recyclers outside your community, look in the yellow pages of a telephone directory under headings, such as Recycling Centers, Waste Reduction, Waste Paper, Scrap Metal, etc., for businesses devoted to salvaging waste. However, it may not be economically wise to spend a lot of time and gasoline to find a far-off recycler. Your best bet is to promote and expand existing programs in your community.

We would like to acknowledge the following organizations for their help. They can help you in your recycling efforts.

Companies and Organizations

Anchor Hocking Glass Company
1115 West Fifth Ave., Box 600
Lancaster, OH, 43130
(614) 687-2531

Browning-Ferris Industries
757 North Eldridge, P.O. Box 3151
Houston, TX 79253
(713) 870-8100
A recycling company that publishes the
Mobius Curriculum: *Understanding the
Waste Cycle, A Recycling and Environmental Education Curriculum for Grades
4 Through 6.*

California Waste Management Board
1020 Ninth St., Suite 300
Sacramento, CA 95814
(916) 320-3330
(Or write your own state environmental
agency for information.)

Corning, Inc.
Business Public Relations Dept.
Corning, NY 14831
(607) 974-4261

Glass Packaging Institute
1801 K St. NW, Suite 1105-L
Washington, DC 20006
(202) 887-4850

INFORM, Inc.
381 Park Ave. South
New York, NY, 10016
(212) 689-4040
A research organization that publishes the
newsletter *INFORM Reports.*

**National Solid Wastes Management
Association**
1730 Rhode Island Ave., NW, Suite 1000
Washington, DC 20036
(202) 659-4613

**New Jersey Dept. of Environmental
Protection**
Division of Solid Waste Management
Office of Recycling
850 Bear Tavern Rd., CN 414
Trenton, NJ 08625-0414
(609) 530-4001
Publications include *A Guide for
Marketing Recyclable Materials.*

Pennsylvania Glass Recycling Corp.
509 N. Second St.
Harrisburg, PA 17101
(717) 234-8091

**Recycle America
Waste Management, Inc.**
3003 Butterfield Rd.
Oak Brook, IL 60521

**U.S. Environmental Protection Agency
(EPA) Office of Solid Waste**
401 M St., SW
Washington, DC 20460
(800) 424-9346 (Solid Waste HotLine)
(Or contact the regional EPA branch
nearest to where you live.) Publications
include *Bibliography of Municipal Solid
Waste Management Alternatives, The
Environmental Consumer's Handbook.*

Regional Glass
Recycling Programs

**California, Washington, Idaho,
Montana, Nevada, Utah, Arizona:**
California Glass Recycling Corporation
5700 Marconi Ave.
Carmichael, CA 95608
(916) 483-8585

North Carolina, South Carolina:
Carolinas Glass Recycling Program
908 S. Tryon St., #2200
Charlotte, NC 28202
(704) 332-2030

Illinois, Indiana, Kentucky, Ohio, Tennessee, Wisconsin:
Central States Glass Recycling Program
770 E. 73 St.
Indianapolis, IN 46240
(317) 251-0131

Arkansas, Colorado, Kansas, Louisiana, Missouri, New Mexico, Oklahoma, Texas:
Mid-America Glass Recycling Program
29 Purfleet Dr.
Bella Vista, AR 72714
(501) 855-4703

Maryland, Virginia, West Virginia, District of Columbia:
Mid-Atlantic Glass Recycling Program
1800 Diagonal Rd., #600
Alexandria, VA 22314
(703) 836-4655

New Jersey:
New Jersey Glass Recycling
Association
P. O. Box 8169
Glen Ridge, NJ 07028
(201) 748-4855
Publications include *The Great Glass Caper*.

Delaware, Pennsylvania:
Pennsylvania Glass Recycling Corp.
509 N. Second St.
Harrisburg, PA 17101
(717) 234-8091

Alabama, Florida, Georgia, Mississippi:
Southeast Glass Recycling Program
P.O. Box 5951
Clearwater, FL 34618
(813) 799-4917

Manufacturers of Craft Products

The author used the following manufacturers' products to create the projects in this book. (Similar products may be substituted.)

Ad Tech: Crafty Magic Melt low-temperature glue gun and glue sticks. *Aldastar:* Puffy Poms. *Aleene's:* tacky glue (gold bottle), thick designer tacky glue (mauve bottle), Right-On gloss sealer. *Aromatics:* potpourri. *DecoArt:* Americana Acrylic paint, Dazzling Metallics gold paint. *Delta:* Ceramcoat acrylic paint, Glitter Stuff gold. *Fairfield Processing Corp.:* Poly-fil. *Felters:* felt. *Fibre Craft Corp.:* "D" ring, brass ring. *Fiskars:* scissors. *Forster:* wooden beads, craft stick. *Loctite Corp.:* hot glue gun and glue sticks. *Marx:* paintbrushes. *McCormick:* food and egg dye. *C. M. Offray & Sons:* ribbons. *One & Only Creations:* Curly Hair, (Maxi or Mini). *Plaid:* Mod Podge. *Wm. E. Wright Co.:* ribbons and laces.

All product names are trademarks or registered trademarks of their respective holders.

Further Reading

Other *How on Earth* books published by The Millbrook Press:

How on Earth Do We Recycle Metal? by Rudy Kouhoupt with Donald B. Marti, Jr.

How on Earth Do We Recycle Paper? by Helen Jill Fletcher and Seli Groves.

How on Earth Do We Recycle Plastic? by Janet Potter D'Amato with Laura Stephenson Carter.

Buy Now, Pay Later! Smart Shopping Counts by Thompson Yardley (Brookfield, CT: The Millbrook Press, 1992).

50 Simple Things Kids Can Do to Save the Earth by J. Jauna (Kansas City, MO: Andrews and McMeel, 1990).

Going Green: A Kid's Handbook to Saving the Planet by John Elkington, Julia Hailes, Douglas Hill, and Joel Makower (New York: Viking Penguin, 1990).

Recycling Glass by Judith Condon (New York: Franklin Watts, 1991).

Re/Uses: 2,133 Ways to Recycle and Reuse the Things You Ordinarily Throw Away by Carolyn Jabs (New York: Crown Publishers, 1982).

What a Load of Trash! Rescue Your Household Waste by Steve Skidmore (Brookfield, CT: The Millbrook Press, 1991).

INDEX

ABOUT THE AUTHORS

Joanna Randolph Rott is a free-lance craft designer, teacher, and certified professional craft demonstrator. She has designed hundreds of projects for books, magazines, and television videotapes. Concern for our environment has led her to develop craft projects from glass objects that we use and discard daily—turning glass trash into glass treasure.

Her long-time association with, and love of, crafting is well demonstrated by her creative designs that challenge children to exercise their imagination.

She is a member of the Society of Craft Designers and lives in Fort Washington, Pennsylvania, with her husband and their three daughters.

Seli Groves, a journalist and syndicated columnist, has created and edited juvenile magazines and written several books. She has always been an active supporter of environmental groups and views recycling as one of the most important and exciting challenges as we rapidly approach the twenty-first century.

She is a member of the American Society of Journalists & Authors, New York Academy of Sciences, and the Society of Children's Book Writers. She is a resident of New York City.